Craig Santos Perez's newest collection is a refusal, as his title testifies, a mutiny. In baring the wounds of American colonialism, the poems expose the simultaneous brutality against Guåhan's physical environment and the CHamoru spirit, concealed beneath a cover of good will, benevolence, and global security. They bear witness.
—Evelyn Flores, co-editor of *Indigenous Literatures from Micronesia*

In Craig Santos Perez's *Call This Mutiny* we are introduced to mutiny in the tradition of lament; mutiny in the tradition of remembering; mutiny that guides the reader to a critical understanding of how indigenous resistance and Pacific life continue to survive against the most hostile of forces. These poems are a rebellion that insist not only on survival but on a seeing that exists beyond naming or mapping; a reminder of the interconnectedness of indigenous struggles across the Americas and the steady power of memory. *Call This Mutiny* teaches us, plainly, that no matter what has occurred "our wounded places/ are the most holy" and it is in that holiness that we revel and thrive!
—Matthew Shenoda, author of *Seasons of Lotus, Seasons of Bone*

Previously Published Works

Poetry

from unincorporated territory [åmot], Omnidawn Publishing (2023)

Habitat Threshold, Omnidawn Publishing (2020)

from unincorporated territory [lukao], Omnidawn Publishing (2017)

from unincorporated territory [hacha], Omnidawn Publishing (2017)
(First edition, 2008)

from unincorporated territory [guma'], Omnidawn Publishing (2014)

from unincorporated territory [saina], Omnidawn Publishing (2010)

Scholarship

Navigating Chamoru Poetry: Indigeneity, Aesthetics, and Decolonization (2022)

Co-edited Anthologies

New Chamoru Literature (2023)
Indigenous Pacific Islander Eco-Literatures (2023)
Indigenous Literatures from Micronesia (2019)
Effigies III: Pacific Islander Women's Poetry (2019)
Geopoetics in Practice (2019)
Home(is)lands: Art and Writing from Guahan and Hawai'i (2017)
Chamoru Childhood (2009)

Call This Mutiny

Cover art and cover design by Craig Santos Perez

Cover typeface: Garamond
Interior typeface: Garamond Premier Pro
Interior design by Craig Santos Perez and Laura Joakimson

Library of Congress Cataloging-in-Publication Data

Names: Santos Perez, Craig, author.
Title: Call This Mutiny : uncollected poems / Craig Santos Perez.
Other titles: Call This Mutiny (Compilation)
Description: Oakland, California : Omnidawn Publishing, 2024. | In English
with some text in Chamorro. | Summary: "Call This Mutiny is the seventh book from
award-winning and internationally-renowned Pacific Islander author Craig
Santos Perez. These poems were originally published in journals and
anthologies between 2008-2023, but this is the first time they have been
collected into a single volume. Throughout, Perez continues his critical
exploration of native cultures, decolonial politics, colonial histories,
and the entangled ecologies of his homeland of Guam, his current
residence of Hawai'i, and the larger Pacific region in relation to the
Global South and the Indigenous Fourth World. As he reminds us about the
power of storytelling: 'If we can write the ocean, we will never be
silenced.'"-- Provided by publisher.

Identifiers: LCCN 2024002660 | ISBN 9781632431288 (trade paperback)
Subjects: LCSH: Colonies--Poetry. | BISAC: POETRY / American / General |
POETRY / Asian / General | LCGFT: Poetry.
Classification: LCC PS3619.A598 M88 2024 | DDC 811/.6--dc23/eng/20240118
LC record available at https://lccn.loc.gov/2024002660

Published by Omnidawn Publishing, Oakland, California
www.omnidawn.com
10 9 8 7 6 5 4 3 2 1
ISBN: 978-1-63243-128-8

Call This Mutiny

Uncollected Poems

craig santos perez

Omnidawn Publishing
Oakland, California
2024

Map of Contents

Dedicated to
Olivia Quintanilla

Ars Pasifika

when the tide

of silence

rises

say

"ocean"

then with the paddle

of your tongue

re-arrange

the letters

to form

"canoe"

Call This Mutiny

to Ferdinand Magellan on the 500-year anniversary of your circumnavigation and arrival to Guam in 1521

my refusal to praise
the first circumnavigation
of the globe,
and to herald your name
bestowed upon
ships, waterways, and galaxies.

Call this mutiny,
       my retelling of the story
from our perspective:
Chamorus standing
on the shores of Guam
sighting three monstrous ships.
They boarded outrigger canoes
and flew towards first contact.

The date: March 6th, 1521,
according to your calendar,
       not ours, in the year
of your Lord, not ours.

Call this mutiny,
       we discovered you
lost and drifting
in our already named ocean,
       we saved you
diseased and starving.

Yet you mistranslated
trade as theft,
branded *us,* "Ladrones."
You disembarked,
burned a village, and killed
seven Chamorus.
   First violence.

Call this mutiny,
my refusal to affirm
that you put Guam
on the map.
You put us in the crosshairs
of empire. Our history
did not begin with your arrival.
   We navigated this sea
long before you ventured
beyond continents.

Call this mutiny,
my refusal to believe
Guam is "Destiny's Landfall,"
that your presence was manifest
by the divine doctrine
of discovery.
   We weren't destined
to be the first colony
in the Pacific,
used as a port
for the galleon trade
between Acapulco and Manila.
We weren't destined
to be baptized
in our own holy blood

by the sharp edge
of the cross.

You called *us* thieves,
        but it was your people who looted
the world. You called *us* savage,
but it was European civilization
that mastered savagery.

Call this mutiny,
because today I commemorate
Guam as *more than a* mere dot
in the latitudes and longitudes
        of imperial history.

I commemorate
the quincentennial
        of Chamorus thriving
beyond the vicious wake
of your voyage.
        I commemorate
Chamoru resilience,
which is so vast
no armada of galleons
        can ever circumnavigate.

Territory

/ˈterəˌtɔri/

t-e-r-ə-t-o-r-ee

T as in take (main stress)
E as in debt
R as in removal
ə as in assault
T as in trespass (secondary stress)
O as in ordnance
R as in settler
e as in colony

The Third Coming
after W. B. Yeats

Dredging and dredging in the widening harbor;
The whales are deafened by navy sonar;
Reefs fall apart; our island cannot hold;
Invasive species are loosed upon the shore,
The bloated sewers are loosed, and everywhere
The day of liberation is celebrated;
Politicians lack conviction, while men
Arrive with predatory investments.

Securely the military binds our hands;
Securely the Third Coming will seize more land.
"No to the buildup!" Protestors shout
As sunburnt tourists take peace selfies.
We stare with horror: in the rising waves,
A shape with eagle body and tip of the spear,
A gaze imperial and merciless as bombs,
Is moving in slow violence, while all around us
flock ghosts of extinct native birds.
The Pivot has begun; *open your eyes*
After a century of colonized sleep,
Awaken to this nightmare in a weapons cradle,
America's war beast, its feeding come round again,
Carriers towards Guam to be berthed.

Benevolence

kill the wild birds

                    save the species

kill the land

                    save the artifacts

kill the chamoru

                    save the soldier

Where America's Voting Rights End

~

My 7th grade social studies teacher
made us memorize the presidents,
whose portraits stared down at us
in the furthest American territory

from the White House.
As I recited their names at home,
my parents watched Bill Clinton
play saxophone on television.

"Are you supporting him?" I asked.
My dad, in his Army t-shirt, said:
"Didn't your teacher tell you we can't vote.
It doesn't matter that we're citizens."

~

Years later, I became a resident
of California and registered to vote.
After Gore lost, I learned living in the states
doesn't guarantee your ballot will count.

I learned how easy it is to remember
a president who wages two wars.
Isn't that what a president is: a name
to which we are ultimately sacrificed.

~

When Barack Obama campaigned, I felt hope
because he's from Hawai'i. But he only visited

Guam once: his plane landed at night
on the air force base, refueled, and departed.

That's when I learned no matter what
the president's name is, he's still
our colonizer-in-chief, and our island
remains an unincorporated name.

~

I didn't vote in the 2016 election,
which felt like a betrayal to my kin
who don't have that privilege.
Activists are now petitioning

to extend voting rights to territories.
But what if we were instead granted
our right to a decolonization plebiscite?
Could we inaugurate genuine liberation?

Memorial Day

Guam has one of the highest enlistment rates among U.S. states and territories, and it has one of the highest concentrations of military veterans. One in eight adults on Guam have served in the armed forces.

America declares federal holiday / we mourn daily

America celebrates three-day weekend / we recite nine-day prayers

America marks beginning of summer / grief is our endless season

America parades / we dust photo albums

America blooms flowers and fireworks / we wilt and ashes

America observes a moment of silence / we miss their voices

America visits national cemeteries / we mass graves

America waves its flags / our flags tightly folded

America sings land of the free / we whisper continent of thieves

America says recruiter's paradise / we...

America dons uniforms / we covered in shrouds

America pledges allegiance / our heartbeats : continuous gun salute

America recounts names of the dead / we count stolen generations

America ignores veterans / we read suicide notes

America commands be all you can be / we ask when will we ever

be whole?

Scorched Earth

Fighter jets scratch contrails across the sky:
                      falcons, eagles, hornets (F-15s, 16s, 18s).
        Machines of prey nest on carrier strike groups.
They call this exercise: *Valiant Shield.*

They call themselves "guardians
                    of nature" and "pioneers of sustainability"
        creating net zero energy bases, hybrid humvees,
                           and biodegradable bullets loaded
            with the seeds of beneficial plants.

But you can't burn 300,000 barrels of oil every day
        and still be a "clean, green fighting machine."
                    Unless by "green," you mean, *money,*
      itself a weapon of mass destruction. Unless by "green,"
you mean "green-washing" and camouflage.

Family Trees

for the 2016 Guam Educators Symposium on Soil and Water Conservation.

Before we enter the jungle, my dad
asks permission of the spirits who dwell
within. He walks slowly, with care,
to teach me, like his dad taught him,
how to show respect. Then he stops
and closes his eyes to teach me
how to *listen. Ekungok,* as the winds
billow the canopy, tremble the understory,
and conduct the wild orchestra.

"Niyok, Lemmai, Ifit, Yoga', Nunu," he says
in a tone of reverence, calling forth the names
of each tree, each elder, who has provided us
with food and medicine, clothes and tools,
canoes and shelter. Like us, they grew in dark
wombs, sprouted from seeds, were nourished
by the light. Like us, roots anchor them here.

"When you take," my dad says, "take with
gratitude, and never more than what you need."
He teaches me the phrase "eminent domain,"
which means "theft," means "to turn a place
of abundance into a base of destruction."
The military uprooted trees with bulldozers,
paved the fertile earth with concrete, and planted
toxic chemicals and ordnances in the ground.
Barbed wire fences spread like invasive vines,

whose only fruit are the cancerous tumors
that bloom on every branch of our family tree.

Today, the military invites us to collect
plants and trees within areas of the jungle
slated to be cleared for impending
construction. Fill out the appropriate forms
and wait 14 business days for a background
and security check. If we receive their
permission, they'll escort us to the site
so we can mark and claim what we want
delivered to us after removal. They say
this is a benevolent gesture, but why
does it feel like a cruel reaping?

Listen, an ancient wind rouses the jungle.
Ekungok, i tronkon Yoga' calls us to stand tall!
Listen, i tronkon Lemmai calls us to spread our arms wide!
Ekungok, i tronkon Nunu calls to link hands!
Listen, i tronkon Ifit calls us to be firm!
Ekungok, i tronkon Niyok calls us to never break!
Listen, i halom tano' yan i taotaomo'na call us
to surround our family of trees and chant,
Ahe'! No! We do not give you permission!

ECL

(English as a Colonial Language)

American authorities
banned
Chamoru to communicate
destiny
English enforced empire's
frontier of "freedom"
Guåhan : *we*
have : home-
island silenced by
jingo of unjust
kkklepto-state
language lost
mouths muted
nouns in
oceanic orature or
pasifika palates
quelled
ravaged by
snakes swallowing
totot...
undercurrent
vowels
wild now
xiled
yoke
zombie tonguez

Home Court

With a basketball tucked under my arm,
I bike to my cousin's house where the neighbors
installed a hoop at the end of the cul-de-sac.

I untuck my Catholic school uniform,
double-knot my sneakers, and dribble around
potholes, loose gravel, and asphalt.

My friends who live nearby join
when they hear the ball bang the wooden
backboard and clang the slack metal rim.

We play for hours, only pausing when a car
drives by, or when auntie yells "dinner,"
or until the sun goes down.

~

One day, a group of boys from other
Micronesian islands migrate to our court.
We divide teams: *us vs. them.*

Shoot for ball. Check. Quickly,
a friendly game becomes competitive.
We screen, box-out. Elbows and hard fouls

lead to angry stares—*game point.*
I don't recall who won. Only that more kept
arriving each day, taking over our space.

~

Weeks later, I bike to my cousin's house.
I dribble the ball around the empty street.
The neighbors took down the hoop.

Micronesians in Denial

"And YES, Guam, the U.S. Territory,
is located in MICRONESIA
And the people there, Chamorros,
are MICRONESIANS in denial"

—Emelihter Kihleng *from* "The Micronesian Question"

Every year, I'd watch the mango tree
in grandma's yard bud.

We picked a few unripe, green fruit,
cut and dipped in salt and soy sauce.

We waited for the others to ripen
into the yellow, orange, and red sunrises
of Micronesia.

Mapmakers named our part of the ocean,
"Micronesia," because they viewed our islands
and cultures as small and insignificant.

Small enough to be colonized by
Spain, England, Germany, Japan, Australia,
New Zealand, the USA. Small enough
to become plantations, church missions,
military bases, phosphate mines,
nuclear testing grounds, detention centers,
and tourist destinations.

Small enough to hide the crimes of empire.

I will never forget the day
all the mangoes were stolen.

"Those criminal Micronesians."
"Those dirty Micronesians."
"Those drunk Micronesians."
"Those welfare Micronesians."

"Go back to where you came from."

Towards the end of the Cold War, an era
of decolonization dawned in Micronesia.
Nauru gained independence in 1968,
Kiribati in 1979. The Northern Marianas
became a US commonwealth in 1978.
The Marshall Islands, Palau,
and the Federated States of Micronesia
(Yap, Chuuk, Pohnpei, Kosrae)
became independent and signed
Compacts of Free Association (COFA)
with the USA in 1986,
which allowed citizens of these new
island nations to migrate, work, and live
as "habitual residents" in the states and territories.
Today, nearly 20,000 Micronesians from
COFA nations have settled on Guam.

Guam has remained a US territory.
One of the last colonies in the world.

Is that why they say Chamorus
are "Micronesians in denial"?
Because we've denied being like
other Micronesians? Because
we've denied the humanity
of *other* Micronesians?

Is that why they say Chamorus
are "Micronesians in denial"?
Because we've been denied our right
to sovereignty?

Dear Micronesian cousins,
Dispensa yu, I'm sorry.
You deserve better.

Dear Micronesian cousins,
so much has been taken
from my people.
No one asked us permission
to turn our island
into an American "horizon."

Dispensa yu, I'm sorry.
We deserve better.

Off-Island Chamorus

My family migrated to California when I was 15 years old.
        During the first day at my new high school, the homeroom
teacher asked: "Where are you from?" "The Mariana Islands,"
        I answered. He replied: "I've never heard of that place.
Prove it exists." When I stepped in front of the world map
                on the wall, it transformed into a mirror: the Pacific

Ocean, like my body, was split in two and flayed to the margins. I
        found Australia, the Philippines, Japan. I pointed to an empty
space between them: "I'm from this invisible archipelago."
        Everyone laughed. And even though I descend
from oceanic navigators, I felt so lost, shipwrecked

on the coast of a strange continent. "Are you a citizen?"
        he probed. "Yes. My island, Guam, is a U.S. territory."
We attend American schools, eat American food, listen
        to American music, watch American movies, play American sports,
learn American history, dream American dreams, and die in American wars.
"You speak English well," he proclaimed, "with almost no accent."

This is what it means to be a diasporic Chamoru:
        to feel foreign in a domestic sense.

Over the last 50 years, we've migrated
        for jobs, schools, hospitals, adventure, and love;
but most of all, we've migrated for military service,
        deployed and stationed to bases around
the world. According to the 2010 census:

44,000 Chamorus live in California, 15,000 in Washington,
        10,000 in Texas, 7,000 in Hawai'i, and 70,000 more
in every other state.

We are the most "geographically
dispersed" Pacific Islander population within the United
            States, and off-island CHamorus now outnumber
our on-island kin, with generations having been born
            away from the Marianas, including my daughters.

Some of us will be able to return for holidays, weddings,
            and funerals; others won't be able to afford
expensive plane tickets. Years and even decades might pass
            between trips, and each visit will feel too short.
We'll lose contact, and the island will continue to change
            until it becomes unfamiliar to us.

This, too, is what it means to be a diasporic Chamoru:
            to feel foreign in our own homeland.

Even after thirty years away, there are still times I feel adrift,
            without itinerary or destination. When I wonder: *What if we
stayed? What if we return?* When the undertow
            of these questions begins pulling us out to sea,

remember: migration flows through our blood
            like the aerial roots of the banyan tree.
Remember: our ancestors taught us how to carry our culture
            in the canoes of our bodies. Remember: our people,
scattered like stars, form new constellations
            when we gather. Remember: home is not simply
a house, village, or island; home is an archipelago of belonging.

Åmot

Eåmtis are Chamoru traditional healers who gathered and prepared plants as åmot (medicine).

the first eåmtis
found me

in the jungle
bowed to my leaves

called me saina
told me stories

about her sick village
i pitied them

prone to illness
and pain

they weep
like no other

wounded animal
on this island

so i gifted her
my body

to soothe
her people

she taught
her daughter

the places i grow
abundant

and *this*
was how we grafted

i taotao
to i tano...

until doctors
and hospitals...

until cancer
and diabetes...

until the descendants
of the first eåmtis

stopped...but now
they're returning

seeding
my names

rooting
the language

of åmot
so that we may grow

perennially
so that we may

once again blossom
and heal

Make-Believe Nation

We drive through industrial Honolulu:
ocean blue tarps and colorful tents
cluster like coral reefs amongst a shipwreck
of shopping carts and bikes. This encampment
is one of many across Hawai'i, the state
with the highest houseless rate. So many islanders
barely surviving beyond the postcard frame.
Families bankrupted by the high cost
of living in *paradise*.

I park at the Children's Discovery Center
and unbuckle my daughter from her carseat.
After I pay admission fees, she pulls me
by the hand to her favorite area: a make-believe
town with a post office, clinic, library, theater,
television studio, grocery store, and classroom.
As she plays, I make-believe a nation
where all this is a public good, non-rivalrous
and inclusive. A nation where housing,
government, and food are no longer privatized.
A nation divested from harmful military regimes.

When we leave, I slowly drive away. Soon,
real bulldozers, dump trucks, and cops
will enforce laws that ban sitting or lying
in public spaces. They'll sweep these makeshift
homes off the sidewalk, where a girl,
who looks the same age as my daughter,
is riding a rusted, green tricycle.

Detour

for Kyle Kajihiro and Auntie Terri Keko'olani

The World War II Valor in the Pacific National Monument

More than a million tourists march
      as "Remember Pearl Harbor" echoes

with patriotic fervor. But what if we mourned
      "Ke Awalau o Pu'uloa," the Hawaiian name

for this place, where watersheds once birthed an estuary
      teeming with spawn, fish, and oysters?

What if we honored Ka'ahupāhau who, in the form of a shark,
      protected this harbor for generations?

What if we were given a map of PACOM
      and toured the 700 toxic Superfund sites here?

What if national parks didn't preserve the myth
      of American innocence,

but actually told the truth
      about American empire?

Would January 17, 1893
      live in infamy?

Aloha Wear(y)

I hate aloha shirts. I hate wearing plumerias, hibiscus, and tiaré because I'm allergic to flowers. I hate wearing pineapples as much as I hate pineapples on my pizza. I hate wearing endangered birds, fish, and turtles because they're going out of style. I hate wearing quilt patterns when it's 90 degrees outside. I hate collars. I hate Santa Claus surfing. I hate wearing boats and helicopters as much as my dad loves watching Magnum PI reruns. I hate fetishizing hula girls. I hate buttons. I hate that Elvis wore a red aloha shirt on his blue Hawai'i album. I hate wearing sunsets and sunrises even more than I hate poems about hope. I hate wearing tiki kitsch as much as tourists love getting drunk in tiki bars. I hate the confusing cultural protocol for aloha shirts. Is it proper to wear an aloha shirt with Japanese lanterns if I'm not Japanese? Or an aloha shirt with Chinese incense sticks if i'm not Chinese? Or an aloha shirt with generic Polynesian motifs if I'm not a generic Polynesian? Or an aloha shirt with Hawaiian tatau if I'm afraid of needles? Is it proper to wear Tori Richards if I'm not a haole? Or Reyn Spooner if I don't work at the Bank of Hawai'i? Or Sig Zane if I'm not a Hawaiian Airlines flight attendant? Is "appropriation" one of the many meanings of "aloha"? Is buying an aloha shirt from Costco less "authentic" than buying an aloha shirt from RIX? I wish someone made a Chamoru aloha shirt featuring latte stones, betel nut, and SPAM. I hate the class hierarchy established by the aloha garment industry. I hate worrying that someone at pau hana will be wearing the exact same aloha shirt I'm wearing. I hate keeping a spare aloha shirt in my car just in case that ever happens. I hate feeling like an unpaid employee of the Hawai'i Tourism Authority dressed in the uniform of paradise. I hate paradise.

Oceanic Men

We are more than what they say we are
We noble chiefs and kings, untouchables and the first baptized
We Kepuha and Mata'pang, Kamehameha and Kalākaua, Tupou
        and Tanumafili
We unite archipelagoes and overthrown
We Tosiwo Nakayama making Micronesia
We John Mangefel reciting a letter from Ngabchai
We Robert Underwood demanding reparations from Congress
We Tony de Brum insisting "1.5 to survive!"
We Frank Bainimarama executing a coup

We are more than what they say we are
We warriors and headhunters
We US Navy mess attendants and the Māori Battalion
We haka before battle
We indigenize soldiering
We fight and die for a nation that colonizes our islands
We UN peacekeepers and private defense contractors
We the fallen brave of Micronesia
We bring the war back to the village
We domestic violence, PTSD, and suicide
We forgotten veterans and uncomfortable fatigues

We are more than what they say we are
We Junior Seau playing defense against concussions and suicide
We Troy Polamalu Head and Shoulders above the rest
We In Football (scholarships) We Trust
We haka before the game
We All Blacks, Manu Samoa, and 'Ikale Tahi
We Jonah Lomu attacking the try in the scrum of his arteries
We USA Sevens Rugby in Las Vegas

We Jabari Parker and Steven Funaki Adams
We All-Mike Basketball Tournaments
We the submission moves of Jon Tuck and BJ Penn
We Yokozuna Akebono using his weight
We the coconut-oiled Olympic flag-bearer that broke the internet
We global sports commodities and disciplined by colonial sports
We beat them at their own games

We are more than what they say we are
We drug dealers, thieves, murderers, rapists, and pimps
We street fights, dog fights, and cock fights
We cops and prison guards
We hula for Makahiki from an Arizona prison
We Joseph Kahahawai wrongly convicted
We Mighty Mongrel Mob, Sons of Samoa, Tongan Crips, USO
        Family, and Hawaiian Syndicate

We are more than what they say we are
We Mau Piailug and Nainoa Thompson guiding us back
We Hokule'a on a worldwide voyage
We Duke Kahanamoku breaking the 100-meter freestyle world
        record in 1911
We *Eddie* (Aikau) *would go*

We are more than what they say we are
We farmers, fishermen, and hunters
We work for Dow and Monsanto
We once were whalers

We are more than what they say we are
We orators, chanters, and storytellers
We speak native tongues and remaster colonial languages
We "Unwriting Oceania"
We *Uncle's Story, Visions of a Chamoru, No Ordinary Sun, The Land*
        Has Eyes, Star Waka, Waimea Summer, Once Were Warriors,
        and *Leaves of the Banyan Tree*
We pidgin, creole, tok pisin and multilingual
We long-winded litanies
We beat them at their own genres

We are more than what they say we are
We John Pule, John "Prime" Hina, and Polyfantastica
We Manny Crisostomo receiving the Pulitzer Prize for his
        photographs of a Detroit school
We Leonard Iriarte and Halau Na Kamalei
We Keanu Reeves, Dwayne Johnson, and Jason Momoa
We Cliff Curtis playing a Black drug dealer, Iraqi rebel, Colombian
        drug lord, Indian self-help guru, Latino FBI director,
        Chicano gangster, and the Fire Nation lord
We Taika Waititi winning an Oscar
We Alex Munoz and the Muna Brothers
We Bruddah IZ, JD Crutch, J Boog, Marianas Homegrown, Fiji,
        Common Kings, and Sudden Rush
We Sig Zane and Fokai
We Tun Jack Lujan forging a machete
We Keone Nunes and Su'a Peter Suluape tatauing the post-colonial
        body

We are more than what they say we are
We AA, BA, MA, MFA, PhD, JD, and MD
We dropouts sinking below grade level
We *Repositioning the Missionary, Racial Crossings, and Cultures of*

Commemoration, Dismembering Lāhui, Native Men Remade,
and "Our Sea of Islands"
We Futa Helu and 'Atenisi
We don't see ourselves in the curriculum so we rewrite the
        curriculum

We are more than what they say we are
We service industries and construction sites
We hotel security and McKinley car wash
We lawyers in designer suits and judges in black gowns
We offshore bankers and business owners
We recruited by Tyson Chicken and Sea World
We entrepreneurs with a cultural purpose
We unemployment checks and eviction notices

We are more than what they say we are
We protect Kahoʻolawe
We Angel Santos and I Nasion Chamoru climbing the military
        fence
We Benny Wenda raising the Morning Star flag
We Jean-Marie Tjibaou and the Kanak Socialist National Liberation
        Front
We Polynesian Panthers
We the Mau movement on Black Saturday
We the voice of George Helm
We climate warriors

We are more than what they say we are
We faʻafafine, māhu, mamflorita, fakaleiti, raerae, and takātapui
We third gender, transgender, and transvestite
We S.O.F.I.A.S. and U.T.O.P.I.A.
We Esera Tuaolo *Alone in the Trenches*
We Coming Out and Overcoming

We are more than what they say we are

46

We worship Ao, Adaro, Afa, Atu, Bakoa, Bue, Dakuwanga Hoa-
        Tapu, Kū, Kāne, Kanaloa, Limu, Lo, Loa, Lono, Maui,
        Nobu, Oro, Puntan, Ra, Rangi, Rua, Tangaroa, Tagaloa,
        Tiki and Tu
We Christians, Catholics, Muslims, Buddhists, Hindis, Mormons,
        Jehovah's Witnesses, and atheists

We eat more than what they say we should
We Spam, Starkist, Vienna Sausage, and Corned Beef
We turkey tails, cheap meats, and flap food
We McDonald's and Zippy's, KFC and Krispy Kreme
We co-founded a "vegan butcher shop" in Minnesota
We EBT cards and foodstamps
We malnutrition and diabetic

We are more than what they say we are
We pure blood, half breed, afakasi, hapa and every fraction in
        between
We every color of sand from black to white
We tall and short, six-pack and beer gut
We kotekas to protect our cocks
We long hair, dreadlocks, topknots, and crew cuts
We bird feathers, face paint, and tribal tattoos
We leave our slippahs at the door

We are more than what they say we are
We migrate to large cities, urban islands, and distant continents
We send remittances and wish we could send more
We dawn raided and deported
We once belonged

We are oceanic men
        shaped by waves
imperfect moving islands

We are more than
what they say we are

Twinkle, Twinkle, Morning Star
West Papua's Flag Raising Day, December 1st

I watch cartoons on my laptop
with my daughter. *How many Papuan*
children are missing their parents?
She sings: "Twinkle, twinkle,
morning star..." I don't correct her.
How many are forgotten refugees,
forgotten birds of paradise?
"...how I wonder where you are..."
I log onto Facebook from my iPhone,
change my profile picture
to a graphic of the West Papua flag.
"...up above mountains so high..."
I share an article about the Grasberg mine.
How many are dying from copper poisoning?
"...like a diamond in the sea..."

Storm Tracking

after cyclone winston after typhoon yutu after hurricane maria after...

this is when a warming ocean
        gives birth to cyclones—
                this is when we give human names
                        to weather we can't control—

this is when the world
        briefly sees us: only after
                the eye of a storm
                    sees us—

this is when counting donations
        becomes prayer—
                this is when counting bodies becomes prayer—

this is when we chant: "we will overcome"

this is when disaster justifies
        militarism—
                    this is when politicians siphon aid
and corporations promise "green development"
                this is when public utilities & schools
        are closed & privatized—

                    this is when we migrate
        with or without dignity—

this is when counting days
        until the next storm

        becomes prayer—
this is when our sea
      of vulnerable islands
         becomes an archipelago
    of prayer—

Disarming

after every mass shooting

Can we be safe
anywhere
if our military
wages endless
wars
everywhere?
Can we control
guns at home
if our government
uncontrollably
sells them abroad?
Can we disarm
our nation
if we don't
demilitarize
our imagination?

Black Lives Matter in the Pacific

Waves of viral images crash against our shore:
Michael Brown's dead body. Armed police in riot gear.

Ferguson, burning. We attend a solidarity rally
in Honolulu. We raise our fists and chant

"Black Lives Matter" into the trade winds.
We praise how the civil rights movement

empowered Pacific decolonization. We praise
the Black Panthers, who inspired Polynesian

panthers. We praise how Black arts and hip hop
inspired new Pacific literature and music.

We raise our fists and recognize this difficult truth:
our islands aren't hospitable, multi-racial paradises.

We stereotype Melanesians, disown mixed-raced
Black Islanders, and discriminate against dark skin.

We raise our fists and I remember the first
Black person I saw on Guam. A soldier

guarding the military gate. Today, African Americans
comprise nearly 20 percent of the armed forces.

We raise our fists and chant "Black Lives Matter."
May we continue to fight for Black equality

and Pacific sovereignty. May we always raise our fists
and chant, "Black Lives Matter," into the trade winds.

Translating Land

"tåno" in Chamorro
"'āina" in Hawaiian
"whenua" in Māori
"fanua" in Sāmoan

"dalka" in Somali
"ardhi" in Swahili
"ilẹ" in Yoruba
"umhlaba" in Zulu

Words translated as "hope"
when our ancestors navigated
ocean and continent.

Words translated as "fertile ground"
when they first planted
roots and seeds.

Until Europeans violently mistranslated

as terra nullius
as property   as resources
as frontier   as raw materials
                                 as *mine, mine, mine*

displaced
across the Pacific

                                 enslaved
                                 across the Atlantic

and we
continue to be

                              dis-

possessed
in the *land*
of the free

our futures
foreclosed
by the low cost
of dying

                         yet

we're not gone
not ghost

dreams planted
in the wild
garden
of our breathing
bodies

from Harlem
        to Honolulu
from the Western Pacific
        to East Oakland
from the South Side of Chicago
to the South Seas
from the inner city
        to the outer atolls
from the streets of Ferguson
        to our sea of islands
from every corner of
our diasporas

                we tenderly translate land
                as all that nourishes us
                all that inherits us
                all that homes us

Somebody Colonized the World

"Who the biggest terrorist?"
—Amiri Baraka, *from* "Somebody Blew Up America"

who broke the sky
who shattered the reef
who planted flags
who who who
who say we heathen and they mission
who covets thy neighbors' lands
who holy water boarded souls
who crucified tongues into prayer
who commits the most sins
who who who
who harpooned whales
who flensed flesh
who captain ahab
who who who
who say we dirt and they clean
who diseased blankets
who syphilis, cholera, influenza, measles, smallpox
who who who
who say we savage and they pilgrim
who slaughtered buffalo
who broke treaties
who mapped trails of tears
who who who
who say we property and they owner
who buys and sells bodies
who kidnapped *blackbirds blackbirds blackbirds*
who who who
who say we labor and they boss

who owns plantations
who profits from cotton, sugarcane, coffee, tobacco, pineapple
who the pesticide load
who who who
who say we ward and they warden
who lies about democracy
who manifests everyone else's destiny
who who who
who say we student and they teacher
who writes the text books
who standardized our minds
who who who
who says we illegal and they law
who built school-to-prison pipelines
who profits from private jails and inmate labor
who rough ride and choke hold
who suicides us by asphyxiation
who never fits the description
who who who
who says we soldier and they commander
who built school-to-military pipelines
who leaks fuel into aquifers
who who who
who bombed vieques, aleutians, kahoʻolawe, kiritimati, pohakuloa,
makua, pagan
who nuclear detonated enewetak and bikini
who fathered jelly babies
who said "there are only 90,000 people out there who gives a damn"
who who who
who say we exotic and they normal
who owns hotels and golf courses
who is never a cheap souvenir
who who who
who loosed mongoose

who waked brown tree snakes
who put fire ants in our plants

who infested coconut trees with rhino beetles
who the most harmful invasive species
who who who
who say we tenant and they landlord
who owns million dollar condos, vacation rentals, eco-luxury resorts
who buys private islands with bitcoins
who who who
who say we accident and they navigators
who owns super yachts
who offshore drilling and deep-sea mining
who say the ocean is their EEZ
who who who
who say we backwards and they progress
who invented NAFTA
who secretly negotiating TPP
who APEC
who killed kollin elderts
who who who
who underwrites
whaling ships, slave ships, tuna ships, shipping ships
who predatory loans and hedge funds
who creditors and vulture capitalists
who who who
who bio-piracy
who transgenic organisms
who GMO seeds
who who who
who master of removal
who master of enslavement
who master of monoculture
who master of extraction
who master of deportation

who master of incarceration
who master of desecration
who master of invasion
who master of extinction
who master of austerity
who master of the century
who master of breath
WHOOOOOOOOOOOOO

Between the Pacific and Palestine

I hold my daughter's hand as we walk
along Waikīkī beach. Nine thousand miles away
in Gaza, Palestinians march for their right of return
and mourn the 70th anniversary of Nakba.
We build sandcastles while their villages
are bulldozed and illegal settlements erected.
We're familiar with the catastrophe that comes
when nations imagine our land as settler paradise.
The United States relocated its embassy
to Jerusalem. Most countries condemned this,
but many independent Pacific states supported it
because they have diplomatic ties with
and receive aid from Israel. Plus, many islanders
are Christian. Today, soldiers killed countless
Palestinians. I see their pictures online.
I say unfamiliar names until they sound like family.
The first: "Laila Anwar Al-Ghandour.
Tear gas inhalation. Eight months old."
How long will we embargo our empathy?
How long will we blockade flotillas
of solidarity between...

The Native Speaks of Toxins
after Langston Hughes

We've known toxins.
We've known toxins ancient as uranium and heavier than the
        flow of blood quantum through less-than-human veins.

Our bodies have grown sick from toxins.

We bathed in Radiation when nuclear dawns were young.
We built homes near Chemical Valley and it choked us to sleep.
We looked upon Polluted Waters and raised our children around it.
We heard the spraying of Glyphosate when Monsanto came to town, and
we've seen the fertile soil
        turn to fugitive dust in the sunset.

We've known toxins.
Modern, cancerous toxins.

Our bodies have grown sick from toxins.

say

mtns r scrd

because mtns are born

from contracting tectonic plates—

because mtns inhabit a quarter of the planet—

because mtns shape climates—*say "mtns r scrd"* because mtns

nourish trees, animals, and crops—because mtns create corridors

for migrating species—because my family lives on submerged mtns—

say *"mtns r scrd"* because mtns capture moisture from the atmosphere—because mtns filter

aquifers and source rivers—because mtns provide freshwater for half of humanity—*say "mtns r scrd"*

because they're always being desecrated by corporations, armies, and nations who clear-cut, remove, detonate,

drill, extract and pollute—*say "mtns r scrd"* because we say stop! this is our center of creation—stop!

this is where we bury and honor our dead—stop! this is where we pilgrimage and worship—stop!

you're hurting our mtn elders—*say "mtns r scrd"* because there was a mtn here

in this deep opened pit—*say "mtns r scrd"* because my daughter loves

playing at mānoa valley park surrounded by the koʻolau mtns—

because one day she'll ask us "what is the tallest mtn

in the world?" we'll tell her, "mauna kea stands

30,000 feet above the ocean

floor

home

of papa and wakea,

earth mother and sky father,

the birthplace of your hawaiian ancestors" —

say "*mtns r scrd*" because we'll have to tell her about

the construction of massive observatories atop mauna kea—

we'll have to explain why scientists yearn to see billions of light years

into space yet refuse to see the sacredness of this place—*say* "*mtns r scrd*"

because we'll tell her about aloha 'āina protectors who halted the groundbreaking,

who blockaded the access road, held hands, and chanted, "ku kia 'i mauna" —

say "*mtns r scrd*" because We are Mauna Kea Lamlam Nakauvadra Popomanaseu Taranaki

Uluru Lata Silisili Panié Orohena Nemangkawi Terevaka Tabwemasana Kao Enduwa Kombuglu

Ngga Pulu Giluwe Haleakala—*say* "*mtns r scrd*" because we'll teach our children

when you feel threatened, hold your palms out, touch your thumbs

and pointers together to form a triangle—*like this*—teach them

when we stand to defend the sacred, we will be as strong

as mountains—and our voices will rise

to the summit of

the sky—

Wounded Places

when they say

our land is

no longer sacred

because

it's been damaged

incrementally

for years—

tell them

our wounded places

are the most holy

Interwoven
Indigenous Peoples' Day

I come from an island
and you come from a continent,
yet we're both made of stories
that teach us to remember
our origins and genealogies.

I come from an island
and you come from a continent,
yet we've both been invaded.
Magellan breached our reef
thirty years after Columbus
raided your shore.

I come from an island
and you come from a continent,
Yet we've both been baptized
in disease and genocide.
We've both been disciplined
by boarding schools, assimilated
by the Western curriculum
of fear and silence.

I come from an island
and migrated to your continent.
Hundreds of thousands of us
settled in your territories.
So busy searching for better lives,
we didn't ask your permission.

We didn't recognize
our American dream
was your American nightmare.

Today, we see you
reviving your cultures,
restoring tribal governments,
planting heritage seeds,
and blockading pipelines.
We acknowledge your land.

I come from an island
that we call a "Blue *Continent*,"
and you come from a continent
that you call "Turtle *Island*."

Let us continue to interweave
our struggles. Let us cultivate
radical hope and decolonial love
so our stories will carry us
towards sovereign horizons.

The Pacific Written Tradition

George Washington High School, Guam, 2010

I read aloud from my new book
to an English class at one of Guam's
public high schools. Afterwards, a student

is crying. "What's wrong?" I ask.
She says, "I've never seen our culture
in a book before. I just thought we weren't

worthy of literature." I wonder how many
young islanders have dived into the depths
of a book only to find bleached coral.

We were taught missionaries were
the first readers in the Pacific because
they could decipher the strange signs

of the Bible. We were taught missionaries
were the first authors because they possessed
the authority of written words.

Today, studies show that islander students read
and write below grade level. "It's natural,"
experts claim. "Your ancestors were an illiterate,

oral people." *Do not believe their claim.*
Our ancestors deciphered signs in nature,
interpreted star formations and sun positions,

cloud and wind patterns, wave currents and
efflorescence. That's why master navigator
Papa Mau said: "If you can read the ocean,

you will never be lost." Now let me tell you
about Pacific written traditions,
how our ancestors tattooed their skin

with scripts of intricately inked genealogies.
How they carved epics into hard wood
with a sharpened point, their hands,

and the pressure of memory.
How they stenciled petroglyphic lyrics
on cave walls with clay, fire, and smoke.

So the next time someone tells you
our people were illiterate, teach them
our visual literacies, our ability

to read the intertextual sacredness
of all things. And always remember:
if we can write the ocean, we will never be silenced.

Acknowledgements

"Ars Pasifika," *Poem-a-Day,* Academy of American Poets, 2020.

"Mutiny," *Alon: Journal for Filipinx American & Diasporic Studies,* 2021

"Where America's Voting Rights End," *Resist Much/Obey Little: Inaugural Poems to the Resistance,* 2017.

"Memorial Day," *Shima* (Australia), 2019.

"Scorched Earth," *NACLA: Report on the Americas,* 2017.

"Family Trees," *Zin Daily* (Croatia), 2017.

"ECL," *The Rumpus,* 2020.

"Micronesians in Denial," *IKA Literary Journal* (New Zealand), 2016

"Off-Island Chamorus," *North Dakota Quarterly,* 2020.

"Make-Believe Nation," *Boston Review,* 2017.

"Detour," *National Endowment for the Arts Imagine Your Parks,* 2016.

"Aloha Wear(y)," *13 Miles from Cleveland,* 2023.

"Oceanic Men," *Gendering the Trans-Pacific World,* 2017.

"Twinkle, Twinkle, Morning Star," *The Hawai'i Review (Wansolwara: Voices for West Papua),* 2015.

"Storm Tracking," Shima Journal (Australia), 2019.

"Disarming," *The Tiny,* 2018.

"Somebody Colonized the World," *Pilgrimage Literary Journal,* 2017.

"The Native Speaks of Toxins," *NACLA: Report on Americas,* 2017.

"Chanting the Mountains," *Siwar Mayu,* 2020.

"Interwoven," *Native Voices: Indigenous American Poetry, Craft and Conversations,* 2019.

"The Pacific Written Tradition," *Cream City Review,* 2016.

Dr. Craig Santos Perez is an indigenous Chamoru from the Pacific Island of Guåhan (Guam). He is the co-editor of eight anthologies and the author of seven poetry collections and the monograph, *Navigating Chamoru Poetry: Indigeneity, Aesthetics, and Decolonization* (University of Arizona Press, 2022).

He earned an MFA in Creative Writing from the University of San Francisco and a Ph.D. in Comparative Ethnic Studies from the University of California, Berkeley.

He has received the National Book Award, the American Book Award, Pen Center USA/Poetry Society of America Literary Prize, Hawai'i Literary Arts Council Award, Nautilus Book Award, and the George Garrett Award for Outstanding Community Service in Literature from AWP. He has also received fellowships and grants from the Lannan, Ford, and Mellon Foundations, as well as from the National Endowment for the Humanities, the American Council of Learned Societies, and the Modern Language Association.

Call This Mutiny
by Craig Santos Perez

Cover art and cover design by Craig Santos Perez
Cover typeface: Garamond
Interior typefaces: Garamond and Garamond Premier Pro
Interior design by Craig Santos Perez and Laura Joakimson

Printed in the United States
by Books International, Dulles, Virginia
Acid Free Archival Quality Recycled Paper

Publication of this book was made possible in part by gifts from
Katherine & John Gravendyk in honor of Hillary Gravendyk,
Francesca Bell, Mary Mackey, and The New Place Fund

Omnidawn Publishing Oakland, California
Staff and Volunteers, Spring 2024
Rusty Morrison & Laura Joakimson, co-publishers
Rob Hendricks, poetry & fiction editor,
& post-pub marketing
Jeffrey Kingman, copy editor
Sharon Zetter, poetry editor & book designer
Anthony Cody, poetry editor
Liza Flum, poetry editor
Kimberly Reyes, poetry editor
Elizabeth Aeschliman, fiction & poetry editor
Jennifer Metsker, marketing assistant
Rayna Carey, marketing assistant
Kailey Garcia, marketing assistant
Katie Tomzynski, marketing assistant
Sophia Carr, production editor